How to be a...

MOUNTAIN BIKING CHAMPION

James Nixon

W
FRANKLIN WATTS
LONDON • SYDNEY

First published in 2015 by
Franklin Watts
338 Euston Road
London NW1 3BH

Franklin Watts Australia
Level 17/207 Kent Street
Sydney NSW 2000

ISBN 978 1 4451 3605 9
Library eBook ISBN 978 1 4451 3607 3

Dewey classification number: 796

A CIP catalogue record for this publication is available from the British Library.

Planning and production by Discovery Books Limited
Managing Editor: Paul Humphrey
Editor: James Nixon
Design: sprout.uk.com
Picture research: James Nixon

Printed in China

Franklin Watts is a division of Hachette Children's Books, an Hachette UK Company.
www.hachette.co.uk

Photo acknowledgements: Cover image (Alamy: Eric Foltz)
Alamy: pp. 4 (epa european pressphoto agency b.v.), 11 top (Oxford Events Photography), 11 bottom (Allstar Picture Library), 12 right (The Photolibrary Wales), 13 top (Wig Worland), 15 top (Malcolm Gallon), 15 bottom (Action Plus Sports Images), 16 (NielsVK), 17 top (Andrew Lloyd), 17 bottom (Seb Rogers), 21 bottom (miscellany), 22 top (epa european pressphoto agency b.v.), 23 bottom (Braden Gunem/ZUMAPRESS.com), 24 (miscellany), 25 bottom (Action Plus Sports Images). Shutterstock: pp. 5 top (Jean-Francois Rivard), 5 bottom (domaniczky), 6 (Gena73), 7 top (Olivier Borgognon), 7 middle (Manczurov), 7 bottom (RioPatuca), 8 top (Vaclav Volrab), 8 bottom (Eric Fahrner), 9 top (Renewer), 9 middle (Jean-Francois Rivard), 9 bottom (Maxim Petrichuk), 10 (Maxim Petrichuk), 12 left (Yaniv Eliash), 13 bottom (mountainpix), 14 (Jean-Francois Rivard), 18 (Jean-Francois Rivard), 19 top (Ljupco Smokovsk), 19 bottom (Jean-Francois Rivard), 20 (Gines Romero), 21 top (Eric Fahrner), 22 bottom (Jean-Francois Rivard), 25 top (Jean-Francois Rivard), 26 (Jandrie Lombard), 27 bottom (A-Babe), 28 left (Jean-Francois Rivard), 28 right (wavebreakmedia), 29 top (R legosyn), 29 middle (Twelve). Wikimedia: pp. 23 top (Graham Dean), 27 top (Courtney Nash), 29 bottom (Aurélien Vialatte).

Every attempt has been made to clear copyright. Should there be any inadvertent omission please apply to the publisher for rectification.

In preparation of this book, all due care has been exercised with regard to the advice, activities and techniques depicted. The publishers regret that they can accept no liability for any loss or injury sustained. When learning a new activity, it is important to get expert tuition and to follow a manufacturer's instructions.

CONTENTS

All words in **bold** can be found in the glossary on page 31

EXTREME BIKING

*Mountain biking is a thrilling form of cycling where riders take their bikes off road on to rough and hazardous **terrain**. To be a mountain bike rider, you need stamina, strength, balance, quick reactions and nerves of steel, especially when you are hammering down rocky trails at high speeds.*

CROSS COUNTRY

Cross-country (XC) mountain biking is a huge test of **endurance**. The riders all start together and set off on a punishing, hilly course full of obstacles. Sometimes races head deep into the wild on narrow trails that wind through forests, mountains, fields or deserts. In 2006, XC mountain biking became an Olympic sport.

DOWNHILL RACING

The other main type of mountain biking is downhill racing. Downhill racers compete on very steep trails on the sides of hills and mountains. The riders have to get from the top to the bottom as fast as possible. Downhill races are **time-trial** events. This means each rider takes it in turn to face the course. The top racers will reach speeds of 60 mph (97 kph) and fly through the air as they hit the jumps.

RAPID ROCKS

Cross-country racers tackle a rocky obstacle during the 2013 Junior World Championships.

ENDURO

There is a third type of mountain bike racing called 'enduro' or 'all-mountain riding'. It is a mixture of downhill and XC. There are sections similar to a downhill course, as well as challenging climbs. Most enduro racers compete for fun, not professionally.

GET ON YOUR BIKE

Wherever you live, there should be trails not far away, where you can ride your bike. Many of the top mountain biking areas are on the edges of cities. Most people ride as a hobby, but once you have built up your fitness and skills, you may want to test yourself in competition. Local mountain bike clubs can be found across the country and always welcome new riders.

RECORD BREAKERS

Steve Peat from the UK is one of the most legendary bikers in the sport. In 2009, at the age of 35, Peat won his 17th Downhill **World Cup** race. This is more World Cup wins than any other rider in history. Peat says... 'Enjoy and have fun. That's all I've done and it seems to have worked out quite well'.

KNOW YOUR BIKE

The range of mountain bikes to choose from is huge. There are hundreds of different designs, all packed with the latest technology. XC racing bikes are very lightweight so they can be ridden fast. Downhill bikes need to be stronger to withstand jumps and drops.

Frame – Mountain bike frames are lightweight, but extremely strong. They are usually made from aluminium tubing, but more expensive bikes are built using **carbon fibre**.

Handlebars – The bars usually rise slightly to give you better control of the bike.

Seat post – The seat post holds the saddle and can be lowered or raised. On downhill sections it is more comfortable to lower the saddle.

Disc brakes – Disc brakes give powerful stopping power. When the brake lever is pressed, pads push against the disc to slow the bike.

Rear suspension – Full suspension bikes have a suspension unit at the rear too.

Suspension fork – The fork absorbs the shock of riding over bumps. The amount your suspension can move is called the 'travel'. Downhill bikes need lots of travel. XC bikes often have front suspension only – these bikes are called **hardtails**.

Gears – XC bikes have up to 30 gears, with three chain rings at the front and ten gears at the rear. Downhill bikes only need one chain ring at the front.

Pedals – Pedals are either 'flat' or hold a fitting that a special bike shoe can clip on to.

Tyres – There are many styles of tyre. Larger, more knobbly tyres grip well in mud and loose terrain. Smoother tyres are quicker on flatter ground.

Whatever bike you choose to buy, it will need regular cleaning.

BUYING A BIKE

Mountain biking is an expensive sport. A decent bike will cost you at least £500. Cheap bikes are not worth the money. They are heavy and the parts wear out quickly. It is also not worth buying a bike that doesn't fit you. A good bike shop will help you find the right bike and make sure that you find it comfortable to ride.

A good starting bike is known as a 'trail' bike. These bikes fall somewhere between XC and downhill bikes. They can climb well and are sturdy enough to tackle most terrain. On a trail bike, you can practise all your skills and decide what type of riding you enjoy the most.

Brake lever

Gear shifter

BIKE CARE

After a ride, a dirty bike needs cleaning. Mud and grit can clog up the bike and damage the parts. Wash the bike down with soapy water using a sponge and a firm brush. WD40 can help to remove grime and stop metal parts from rusting. When the bike is dry, apply fresh **lube** to your chain to keep the bike running smoothly.

It is important to look after a bike's chain to stop it rusting and to keep the gears in good working order.

THE GEAR YOU NEED

Just like choosing the right bike, wearing the right gear is important. The correct gear will keep you safe and comfortable.

HELMETS

Crashes are common, so a helmet is vital and could even save your life. Modern helmets are very light and have lots of **vents** so that you don't get too hot. For downhill riders, full-face helmets with a jaw guard are essential because of the extra protection you need.

BODY ARMOUR

Body armour is a must for downhill racing. Armour includes knee and elbow guards, upper-body plates to protect the spine and padded clothing.

GLOVES

Gloves are a key piece of kit. Riding with gloves on is much more comfortable and gives you better grip. Padded palms also protect your hands when you hit the ground.

GOGGLES

In mountain biking you get a lot of **debris** thrown up at your face. XC racers wear special glasses to protect themselves from dust and grit. Downhill riders wear goggles with their helmets.

XC helmets have lots of vents to keep your head cool.

Full-face helmet

Goggles

Knee pads

SHOES

Mountain biking shoes have stiff soles so that your power is transferred to the pedals. The shoes look like beefed up trainers. They have grippy soles so that your feet don't slip off the pedals. Other bike shoes have **cleats** in the soles, which can clip you in to some pedals.

Mountain bike shoes often have Velcro straps.

TOP DOG

The Olympic Men's XC champion in 2012 was Czech rider Jaroslav Kulhavy (left), beating Switzerland's Nino Schurter by just one second! In 2014 Kulhavy won the Mountain Bike Marathon World Championships. Marathon races are gruelling events that can be up to 160 kilometres (100 miles) long or more, across mountainous terrain.

CLOTHING

Clothing should be comfortable and lightweight. Unless you are a professional XC racer, who wears tight-fitting clothing made from Lycra, you will probably want something more casual. There are lots of casual clothes in the shops designed specifically for mountain bikers.

If you are heading into the wild, take a small rucksack to hold your emergency kit.

INTO THE WILD

On long rides in the wilderness, you should always carry a map, phone, plenty of food and water and waterproof clothing in case the weather turns bad. It is safer if you ride with a friend. You may also need to make some running repairs so make sure you take a basic toolkit, including a mini pump and puncture repair kit.

BASIC SKILLS

There are basic skills to riding a mountain bike that all beginners must learn. Getting these techniques perfect will help you tackle the toughest trails.

ON THE MOVE

Try to pedal in smooth circles, rather than stamping on the pedals. Keep your upper body still or you are wasting energy. Move through the gears to find the easiest and quickest way to pedal.

On a climb, you need to select a low gear. The lower gears are the larger cogs at the back. Make sure you move into the correct gear before you start climbing so that you don't come to a grinding halt.

For riding downhill use a higher gear. You will be able to go much faster. The high gears are the small cogs at the back. For a smooth change of gears, take some pressure off the pedals as you shift. Most of the time riders use the middle ring at the front. On very steep hills, shift into the small ring at the front, and on ultra-fast descents use the big ring.

On a climb you may need to move the chain onto the small ring at the front. This is known as the 'granny ring'.

Basic skills such as braking and cornering become easier the more you practise.

BRAKING

On a fast, rugged trail, try to get into the habit of covering the brake levers with two fingers so that you can react quickly to obstacles. As you brake, squeeze the levers gently. If you pull too hard, the wheels will lock up and skid. Slamming the front brakes on is especially dangerous as you could fly over the handlebars! It's a good idea to shift your weight backwards as you brake to stop yourself being thrown forward.

CORNERING

As you approach a bend, reduce your speed before you turn. Braking during a corner makes the bike much harder to control. Tilt the bike slightly into a fast bend, but keep your body upright with your weight on the outside pedal. As you exit the corner, straighten up, and start pedalling hard again. On slow, tight corners you need to turn the handlebars more. These put your balancing skills to the test.

TOP DOG

Catherine Pendrel from Canada is proof that if you work hard you can make things happen. When Pendrel first started mountain biking, she remembers being nervous on downhills and crashing a lot. Today, she is one of the world's top XC riders. In 2010 and 2012 she won the World Cup. In 2011 and 2014, she claimed the World Championships, and at the Glasgow Commonwealth Games in 2014 she took home the gold medal.

AT THE TRAIL CENTRE

One of the first things you should do when you buy a mountain bike is find your local trail centre. Trail centres are the best places to practise your skills. They contain a mixture of natural and man-made trails to give you the perfect mountain biking experience.

FOLLOW THE TRAIL

Most trail centres are free to use and have **waymarked** routes for riders of all abilities. Routes marked in green are for **novices**. The blue routes are a step up in difficulty, and use more testing and narrow trails. Red routes are longer, steeper and rougher. The black routes are downhill courses. Some centres provide an **uplift** service, which provides the downhill riders with some form of transport to the top of the hill.

Riders at a trail centre decide which route they are going to tackle.

At trail centres, lots of **berms** are built to make the course fast and flowing.

A rider is ready in the 'attack' position.

BY DESIGN

Trail designers build lots of obstacles in to the tracks to make the ride fun and challenging. These include big, banked corners called berms and rollercoaster sections called rollovers. Tight, **switchback** corners are often built on the climbs. Downhill tracks feature lots of rock steps, drops and ramps for jumps.

ATTACK!

At a trail centre, the obstacles can come thick and fast. By putting yourself in the 'attack' position, you will be ready for anything. To do this, raise yourself slightly out of the saddle, and bend your arms and knees with the pedals level. Now you can shift your weight about quickly, and absorb all the trail's bumps. The trick is to have a firm grip on the bars, but stay relaxed. Look and plan ahead, cover the brakes with your fingers, and let the bike float beneath you.

RECORD BREAKERS

Downhill rider Markus Stockl from Austria set a new world speed record in 2011 on a non-**customised** mountain bike. He clocked 102.5 mph (165 kph) on gravel, on the side of a volcano in Nicaragua! In 2013 Frenchman François Gissy reached a record speed of 163 mph (263 kph), but he did have a rocket attached to the bike!

SLAYING SINGLETRACK

Singletrack is a trail that is wide enough for only one bike at a time. Hazards such as rocks and roots cannot be avoided. This is when your balance and bike handling skills are tested to the max. These tips will get you through clean and in control.

CHOOSE YOUR LINE

Riding a singletrack trail is all about planning ahead. Don't keep your eyes fixed down on your front wheel. Keep your head up to spot obstacles that need to be avoided. The faster you are going, the further you need to look down the trail. Look for the best line that has the most grip. The sooner you choose your line to ride, the faster you can go.

RIDING ROOTS

Tree roots are tricky, slippy and catch out many riders. Try to hit the root square-on if possible and get your wheel over it quickly. By hitting a root side-on you are likely to slide out of control.

Some sliding is bound to happen, but don't panic. Relax, let the bike move underneath you, and keep your front wheel on the right line. Stay off the brakes. With so little grip even the slightest pull on the brake lever will send you to the ground.

By keeping your sights on the trail ahead, a slide on a tree root won't feel bad, and you won't tense up.

ROCK GARDENS

Rocky sections called rock gardens are a common part of downhill and XC courses. Racers must carry as much speed over them as possible. Judge your speed into the rocks so that you can accelerate over them. Stay relaxed and aim to keep your upper body as still as possible. Your legs and arms should do all the work, bending to absorb the bumps. The pros make it look easy. They appear to flow like water down the hill.

SPLIT 1

Riders try to choose the best line through a rock garden.

TOP DOG

Englishman Gee Atherton was ranked World Number 1 for downhill mountain biking in 2013. The 2008 and 2014 Downhill World Champion won his first World Cup race in 2004 aged just 19, and has finished in the top five in the overall World Cup standings every year since. Atherton's riding style is spectacular as he attacks the course with breathtaking force, going for lines that many riders would see as technically impossible.

TRAIL TIPS

The greatest challenge of mountain biking is handling anything that the trail throws at you. On top of obstacles, trails can be windy and bumpy, while the ground beneath you can be loose and stony, or damp and boggy.

RIDING BERMS

Banked turns (berms) are not always easy, but they can help you hit corners hard and fast. The banks push back against the tyres, giving you more grip. Even the smallest berms can give you more control, so always be on the lookout for them.

The trick is to ride and push into a berm in the opposite direction to the curve. At the same time lean your body towards the inside of the corner. Stay relaxed and keep leaning all the way through the berm. As you exit the berm, bring the bike back underneath you and power out of the turn with more speed than you came in with.

RIDING BUMPS

From the attack position (see page 13) it is easy to react to bumps in the trail. Keep your head level and work your legs and arms to absorb the bumps. But don't force it – stay loose. As you hit a bump, allow the handlebars to come towards you. Once the front wheel is on top of the bump, push the handlebars forward and down.

On bigger obstacles, you may need to raise yourself out of the saddle more and extend your legs, so that you have a wider range of movement to absorb the bump.

You can use berms to help you ride corners faster.

LOOSE TERRAIN

Sections with loose stones can be the scariest bits of trail. The best tip is to go with the flow and relax, again letting the bike move beneath you. Control your speed on smoother pieces of track and then let go of the brakes through the rougher sections. If you have to brake in the rough stuff, use the back brake gently, because there is little grip and the bike will slide.

Braking needs to be done carefully in loose, stony sections.

MUD AND BOGS

In winter, dry dusty trails can turn into a muddy mess. Slippery conditions mean you have to be even more careful on the brakes. Stick to braking in straight lines on firmer sections. If the wheel starts to skid, let go of the brake immediately. On muddy rides, you should change to a set of tyres with a bigger **tread**.

If you come across a thick piece of bog, don't charge into it full speed, hoping for the best. The last thing you want to do is topple off and get wet. Slow down before the bog, select a low gear and ride through steadily, keeping your knees and elbows relaxed.

Stay relaxed and keep it steady as you ride through bogs.

BEATING GRAVITY

The top mountain bikers can ride impossible-looking climbs and descents. Here are some tips to show you how it is done.

CLIMBS

No matter how fit you are, better climbing technique will save you time and energy. On hard, steep climbs, select a gear early that will get you all the way to the top. If you try to change gears halfway up, you will lose speed. Picking the right line is vital. Look for grippier parts of the trail that will help your ascent.

On hard slopes you should usually stay seated, keeping your weight over the rear wheel. This stops your rear wheel spinning. However, another problem is the front wheel lifting into the air as you pedal. To stop this happening, perch forward on the nose of the saddle and lower your shoulders over the bars. Riders have to constantly shift their weight forwards and backwards in a balancing act. If a climb is short and you hit it fast, you can stand out of the saddle to power up it.

You can get out of the saddle to power up short, sharp climbs.

GOING DOWN

On steep descents, you need to move your hips back towards the rear of the saddle. Again, it is a balancing act. If you hang too far back off the bars, and take weight off the front wheel, you will lose grip and control. Move your weight back as you brake and apply the brakes with great care.

You can keep holding the brakes gently (called dragging) to ease your way down the steepest sections. Remember to stay relaxed, so you are loose and ready to move your weight where it needs to be.

STEEP CORNERS

Steep, tight bends on descents cause a lot of problems. Take a wide line so you don't have to turn as much. The biggest mistake is to approach too fast. The top riders almost come to a standstill before letting go of the brakes and using gravity to carry them through and over the next section.

When riding downhill, keep your weight back towards the rear of the bike.

RECORD BREAKERS

Julien Absalon from France is widely regarded as the greatest XC mountain biker of all time. He has been overall winner at the World Cup series a record six times, winning 29 World Cup races in the process. He has also won the World Championships five times – more than anyone else – and was Olympic champion in 2004 and 2008.

Julien Absalon takes a wide line on a steep, downhill corner.

STEPS AND JUMPS

Steps and jumps are common obstacles on downhill courses. Here are some hints on how the pros make it look so smooth.

ROLL WITH IT

Small steps up to 50 cm high can be rolled off with good technique. Check the line you want to take beyond the step before you go for it. As the front end drops over the edge, allow the bike to fall away from you. Stay loose and bend your knees to lower your body. As the rear wheel starts down the step, extend your legs and pull up on the handlebars to level the bike. The bigger the drop, the more speed you need to stop the chain ring catching on the edge of the step.

DROP-OFFS

Most people ride around large rock drops. However, the pros will take a straight line and fly off the drops. It's all about timing. As you reach the drop at speed, push off the handlebars, moving your shoulders up and back. At the same time, drive the pedal forwards away from you. This will lift the front wheel up to help you clear the obstacle. As your rear wheel leaves the drop, shift your weight forwards to land with both wheels at the same time.

A downhill racer flies off a steep drop.

THE BUNNY HOP

Downhill racers are constantly making small hops to skip over and iron out awkward bits of trail. To bunny hop, crouch low down from the 'attack' position, with your arms and legs bent. Then spring upwards, lifting both wheels off the ground with your arms and legs. To hop sideways, twist your arms and shoulders as the front wheel lifts. Hopping sideways is a great way to avoid obstacles at the last moment.

JUMPS

Jumps are a spectacular part of downhill racing. As you line up for the jump, **compress** your body and push your bike into the ground. At the lip of the jump, stay relaxed and shift your weight back slightly to lift the front wheel. Don't try too hard and avoid pulling up on the bars. Let the back wheel roll all the way to the lip to get maximum lift. When you are in mid-air, push the nose down to level the bike, and absorb the shock of landing with your knees and elbows.

Mastering the bunny hop is a crucial skill for mountain bike racers.

For big jumps, let your back wheel roll all the way to the top of the ramp.

ON LOCATION

The biggest events in XC and downhill mountain biking are the World Cup series and the World Championships – a one-off race each year to find the best in the world. Professional riders travel the globe as they battle for glory.

The Junior event gets underway at the 2013 World Championships in South Africa. The start of a XC race is always important as the riders battle to be at the front before the singletrack starts.

WORLD CHAMPIONSHIPS

The first ever mountain bike World Championships were held in 1990, in the mountains of Durango, Colorado in the USA. Americans Ned 'Deadly Nedly' Overend and Julie Furtado were the cross-country victors. The course can still be ridden today, along with 3,220 kilometres (2,000 miles) of other trails at Durango.

The 2013 World Championships were held in Pietermaritzburg in South Africa, on a fast-flowing dry, dusty course that also holds rounds of the World Cup. Nino Schurter of Switzerland and Julie Bresset of France won the Men's and Women's event. The World Championship winners get the honour of wearing a rainbow-coloured jersey for the next year.

Julie Bresset wears the rainbow-coloured jersey after becoming World Champion.

OLYMPICS

For many XC racers, the ultimate goal is to become Olympic champion. At London 2012, a new XC course was built just outside London especially for the event. The course was gruelling with lots of climbs, many of them containing tight, switchback corners to stop the riders finding their rhythm. Even the fast sections were peppered with rocky obstacles such as rock gardens and drop-offs.

SPONSORSHIP

Travelling across the world and riding the latest technology is an expensive business. To get to the top, you need **sponsorship** to help you with the costs. Contact local shops and bike-gear manufacturers to see if they can help. They will want to know the races you plan on entering and your results. The best thing you can do is to start winning races!

TOP DOG

Rebecca Rusch from Idaho, USA, is one of the world's top endurance mountain bikers. Also known as 'the Queen of Pain', Rusch has won many of America's toughest marathon races, including the Leadville Trail 100 and the Dirty Kanza 200, plus the 24-hour Mountain Bike World Championships. The famous Leadville race in Colorado heads 80 kilometres (50 miles) out of the town and back again. By the finish, the riders have climbed nearly 3,500 metres. When she is not racing, Rusch works as a firefighter in her local town!

DOWNHILL VENUES

The downhill course at Fort William contains huge jumps.

The Downhill World Cup is held every year across a series of events around the world. At each event, riders pick up points by finishing the track as fast as possible. The courses take between just two and five minutes to complete. The gaps between the riders are just a matter of seconds, so there is no margin for error!

SCOTTISH EPIC

The downhill course near Fort William in Scotland is one of the longest and toughest in the World Cup series. At the top, your arms and legs take a pounding as you try to hang on through the endless rocks and boulders. Then the track dips into the forest and becomes very steep and twisty. Huge tree roots and the thick Scottish mud make it even more challenging. After that, you can pedal to the max as you rush down the course to hit four massive jumps before the finish.

RECORD BREAKERS

The length of Fort William's course gives it its fearsome reputation. The record run is held by South Africa's Greg Minnar, with a time of four minutes 35 seconds. In that time the rider drops nearly 600 metres!

TOP DOG

US superstar Aaron Gwin only started racing downhill mountain bikes when he was 20. Just three years later in 2011 he became World Cup Champion and in 2012 he was victorious again. A lot of his style and skill comes from his younger days when he raced BMX bikes. The key to Gwin's success is preparation. He tries to remember every turn and even every rock of each course.

THE ITALIAN JOB

Val di Sole's downhill course in northern Italy is considered to be the biggest test of mountain bike skill. The terrifyingly steep **gradient** is covered in never-ending rocks, roots and sharp turns. Riders must forget that the course has seen many crashes and broken bones and ride without fear. In fact, the riders enjoy racing here, as there are always thousands of screaming Italian fans lining the course.

A racer slides around a sharp corner on the Val di Sole course.

LIFE IN THE SADDLE

NINO SCHURTER

28-year-old Nino Schurter is currently the world's top XC rider. In 2013 he pulled off the 'double', winning both the World Championships and the World Cup.

Schurter was born and grew up in a small village in the Swiss mountains. He spent most of his free time enjoying nature and outdoor activities. Schurter, along with his father and brother, became fascinated by mountain bikes and quickly developed his riding techniques. At 7 years old Schurter entered a local race and won in his category. It was then that he knew he had a special talent.

INTO THE BIG TIME

Schurter did downhill races for a while, but liked XC better because of the all-round skills he could show. After winning lots of Swiss races, he joined a professional team, entering and winning his first ever international competition, the 2004 European Junior Championships. In 2007 he turned professional himself, and has won three World Championships and three World Cups since 2009. At the 2012 Olympics, he was pipped in a sprint finish by Jaroslav Kulhavy and won silver.

Nino Schurter, on his way to winning his first World Championships in Canberra, Australia, in 2009.

RACHEL ATHERTON

Britain's Rachel Atherton has dominated women's downhill racing in recent years. Like Schurter, she won the World Championships and World Cup in 2013.

Atherton began riding BMX at the age of 8 and switched to mountain biking when she was 11. It was clear straight away she had something special, winning junior races wherever she raced. Atherton followed her brothers, Dan and Gee (see page 15), by turning pro in 2005. She says watching them gave her the confidence to try things for herself. In 2008, at just 20 years old she won both the rainbow jersey and the World Cup, a feat she repeated in 2013.

BOUNCING BACK

Injuries are a common part of downhill racing. However bad luck struck Atherton when she was training on a road bike. She got hit by a truck and dislocated her shoulder, which put her out of the whole 2009 season. Atherton came back stronger than ever, winning the first World Cup race in 2010. She is now the most successful British mountain biker in history with 21 World Cup race wins and three World Cup overall wins to her name. She believes that if you go with your instinct you can always push harder and race faster.

Rachel Atherton is not afraid to soar into the air as she makes a winning return to World Cup action after her shoulder injury.

TRAINING AND FITNESS

The top mountain bikers do a lot of training to become super-fit athletes. You may not think it, but even downhill racers train hard for extra power, balance and strength.

TRAIN TO WIN

It might sound obvious, but riding mountain bikes is the best way to train. It's fun, and as well as building your muscles, it strengthens your heart and lungs. Controlling your bike over rough ground is also a great workout for your back, belly, shoulders, neck and arms. Find new trails to ride to keep it fresh and practise riding in difficult conditions. This will improve your skill level quickly.

GETTING FASTER

Make a note of your times on a local loop, so you can see how you are improving. You can then set yourself goals to ride faster. If the weather is very bad you can go swimming or to the gym. Working with weights or using a rowing machine will improve your upper body strength.

Putting in lots of hours on the bike is the best path to success.

Mountain bike riders need strength in their upper bodies as well as their legs.

FOOD AND DRINK

Top bikers are careful about what and when they eat. It's important to fill yourself up the night and morning before a ride. **Carbohydrates** are your main source of fuel, so plenty of pasta is a good option. But don't eat heavy meals just before you race. Energy needs to be replaced as you ride. If you start to feel hungry, eat a banana or an **energy bar** and swill it down with water.

Riders also lose water from their bodies as they ride. Water loss equals a loss in performance, so keep sipping your drink. After a ride, your body quickly needs more carbohydrates to recover. Lean meats such as chicken and fish are also important as a source of **protein** to fuel your muscles.

Pasta is a good source of energy if you are fuelling up for a race or recovering after a long ride.

RECORD BREAKERS

Nicolas Vouilloz from France is a legend of downhill racing. He has won the World Championships ten times! After three wins in the junior category, Vouilloz won the Men's Championship a record seven times between 1995 and 2002.

FIND OUT MORE

BOOKS

Adrenalin Rush: Mountain Biking,
Anne-Marie Laval, (Franklin Watts 2013)

Get Outdoors: Mountain Biking,
Paul Mason, (Wayland 2010)

Mastering Mountain Bike Skills,
Brian Lopes and Lee McCormack, (Human Kinetics Publishers 2010)

Mountain Biking Skills Manual,
Alex Morris, (J H Haynes & Co 2011)

WEBSITES

www.mtbtechniques.co.uk
How to improve your mountain biking skills and techniques

www.bikeradar.com/mtb/gear/article/how-to-ride-trail-centres-30174
This site has guides on how to ride trail centres, what to eat, what bike to buy and much more

www.wikihow.com/Category:Mountain-Biking
A series of 'How to…' guides for mountain bike owners

www.moredirt.com/mtb_trails.php
All the information you need to plan your next mountain bike trip

www.singletracks.com/channels/beginners
Advice and articles for mountain biking novices

www.uci.ch/mountain-bike/news
Find out the latest professional mountain biking results

Website disclaimer: Note to parents and teachers: Every effort has been made by the Publishers to ensure that these websites are suitable for children, that they are of the highest educational value, and that they contain no inappropriate or offensive material. However, because of the nature of the Internet, it is impossible to guarantee that the contents of these sites will not be altered. We strongly advise that Internet access is supervised by a responsible adult.

GLOSSARY

berm a banked corner, usually made entirely of dirt

carbohydrates a group of foods that can be broken down to release energy in the body

carbon fibre an extremely strong and light material, in which several thousand fibres of carbon are bonded together in crystals

cleat a metal piece attached to the bottom of a shoe, which clips into a special bicycle pedal

compress squeeze into less space like a coiled spring

customised altered radically so that it looks unlike anything produced in a factory

debris loose material such as stones and dirt

endurance the ability to continue when something is hard, tiring or painful

energy bar a bar containing cereals and other high energy foods, for people that require quick energy but do not have time for a meal

gradient the sloping part of a track or road

hardtail a bike with suspension at the front end, but not the rear

lube a substance used for greasing (lubricating) a part of a machine

novice a beginner

protein one of the building blocks of muscles and an essential fuel for the human body

sponsorship funding for a sportsperson's costs in return for advertising

switchback a corner that bends back sharply so that you end up facing the opposite direction

terrain the features of a piece of land

time trial a test of a competitor's speed over a set distance

tread the part of a tyre that grips the track

uplift a way of transporting your bike to the top of a hill

vent a slit that allows air to pass out

waymarked containing a series of signs to mark a route

World Cup a series of mountain bike races held at courses around the world. Riders win points according to their placing in each event, which are added up to decide the overall winner.

INDEX